Dedication

To my husband (Ronald), our children (Kennetta, KieVonne, Krystal, Ceno, and KJ - Man of God), and our beautiful grandchildren, you are some of the reasons why I am affirming my way to A Better Me.

Acknowledgments

I am so grateful to be called out of darkness into the Lord's light. I love living my life in Christ. Thank You, Father God, for loving me without condition and leading me by Your Spirit to the Rock that is higher than I.

Ronald, there is no space nor is there enough time to write my words of appreciation and love for you. When I say you bring it, you get it. I love doing life with you. Glad to call you hubby, friend, ministry and business partner, a great father, Papi, Bishop, and so much more.

Kennetta, KieVonne, Ceno, Krystal, and KJ - Man of God. I love you all deeply, and each of you is my favorite. God blessed me with the right children. #mommylove #strongbond #foreverfamily

To our seventeen17 grandchildren – both Papi and I love each of you. We cannot convey the measure of joy we have in our hearts and the gratitude we have for God and your parents for blessing us with each of you. Life with you is simply amazing. #omalove #mydoover #wegotyourback

To my brothers, I am grateful for our bond and the love we have for one another. Your families have a special place in my heart. I thank God for you all. And to Shirley and Deborah, my husband's sisters, who are my sisters too – love, love you. I thank all of you for your prayers.

Refreshing Lives Church -- On this other side of "Yes, Lord", together we can do it. Love serving you and watching you grow. I am honored to be one of God's under-shepherds for your life. Everyone deserves to live a refreshing life!

THE REVISED VERSION OF

Affirming My Way to a Better Me

You Say It

ANGELA M. SCOTT

The Revised Version of Affirming My Way To A Better Me: You Say It

PASTOR | MASTER CERTIFIED LIFE COACH | HOLISTIC HEALTH COACH AND CONSULTANT
Angela M. Scott
A Better Me Empowerment
www.itsabetterme.org.
contact@itsabetterme.org
Social Media: A Better Me Empowerment

Some names and identifying details have been changed within this book to protect the privacy of the individuals.

Unless otherwise noted, all Scripture quotations are taken from YouVersion Bible Application.

ZCP

Zyia Christian Publishing, LLC
zyiachristianpublishing@gmail.com

Distributed by IngramSpark.

Printed in the United States of America.

ISBN: 979-8-218-18445-2

10 9 8 7 6 5 4 3 2

To my dearest friends, though the circle is small, it is fierce, and I thank God for you.

ABME Planning Team (Keda Pullins, Jasmine Warthen, Mickey Smith and Shaunda McKinnon) – You are amazing, and your partnership, collaboration, cohesiveness, unity, and the love that we have for one another is priceless. Thank you for taking the time to understand the vision, and to, with liberality, assist in bringing it to past.

22999ers – You are a fantastic group of men and women! As you can see, some of your affirmations made it into this book. Thank you for being a part of the community.

Big thank you to Nyisha D. Davis (The Book Birthing Midwife), my publisher. Working with you is like stroking a canvas to create something beautiful that all who encounter the finished product are touched and moved by. Thank you for your professionalism, and commitment in seeing my projects completed with excellence.

To the wonderful medical professionals who have stood in faith with me and my family, and served with the wisdom of God, thank you.

Numbers 6:24-26 (GWT)

The Lord will bless you and watch over you. The Lord will smile on you and be kind to you. The Lord will look on you with favor and give you peace.

Table of Content

A BETTER ME EMPOWERMENT
A BETTER ME IS FOR YOU SM

Introduction

Had this book been published before the COVID-19 pandemic, I can assure you that it would have required me to rewrite it. So much has happened in 2020, but let me say that not all of it was bad, though it may have seemed to be. Now that it is 2023, at the republishing of this book, we are further on the other side of it. I pray that what we witnessed during the pandemic we will not ever experience again.

There are some things that I lived through, witnessed, embraced, and celebrated, during this same period. It was not because of what I went through, but the willingness and preparation to see change. My most significant level of victory, overwhelming success, has always resulted because I chose not to doubt God's Word or my ability to apply the Word of God. Additionally, I diligently, throughout the day, spent time affirming my way until I saw manifested in my life what I saw on the canvas of my imagination. As a result, I am A Better Me.

Things are so different on this segment of my life journey than other segments and times I was striving to be better. It was not that the progress did not work, and it was not that I did not see the manifestation. However, the focus was narrow. Therefore, the successes, though significant, were not as in-depth as they could have been. You will hear more about that in other chapters.

As we assess who we are, and the commonality that exists between us all, we are spiritual beings having an earthly experience. Spirituality is a permanent fixture of our lives, no matter our beliefs. There is also a mental component to each of us — whether we are whole, fractured, or in need of intense therapy. Of course, there is a physical component to us, we can agree, and it too needs to be cared for as it is a permanent fixture of our life. Let us not forget about the social component, that to some degree now includes social media. And the final permanent fixture to our life is financial literacy and empowering our money versus being a slave to it.

Well, with the five areas being significant to our existence and well-being, we must learn and be disciplined to put some skin in the game in all areas, though the degree may vary based on our priorities. So, we should challenge ourselves to be better in every segment, and not just live within one particular space, and this book demonstrates one of the ways we can all do that by affirming every area of our lives. After all, a better me is for you and me. And, my commitment to putting the work in has thus far yielded fruit of me being a better me.

Me being A Better Me is in no way an indication that I have finally arrived. No instead, I want you to see it as purposing to be better on each level of my life, in every area of my life, with the help of God, because better is for me. Just as it has not only worked but is still working for me, I declare that your will to live better and your actions to achieve better will produce results as you too say, ***Affirming My Way to A Better Me***. You say it.

Part 1

A Better Me Spiritually

As I said in the introduction, no matter what or who you believe in, everyone is a spiritual being living in an earth suit. There was a time in my life when I had limited knowledge and understanding about the spiritual being component. Growing up, I believed there was a God. However, I did not know that He was/is approachable, loving, compassionate, forgiving and so much more. I had to learn about the positive and wonderful attributes of God.

One day, I remember feeling weighted down and empty. I knew that there had to be better for me. So on my limited knowledge and lack of relationship with God, I decided to pray to Him and ask Him to change me. When I invited Jesus into my heart, I was not in front of a church, a group of people, or out in the public where someone handed me a track to talk to me about Jesus (though I do not think that there is anything wrong with any of that).

Instead, I went to my bedroom, fell on my knees, and asked Jesus to come into my heart. That is where it all began. The weighted-down feeling lifted, and the emptiness went away. From that day to this, for me, Jesus is REAL. From the day I accepted Christ, I have always believed that this is one of the most rewarding, eternal, empowering, and fruitful decisions I have ever made. And though I was assured and confident that

I could trust God's Word, I lacked a relationship with Him, so I pursued one. This decision became an eternal turning point.

Manifestations of Better

As a believer, I have had numerous manifestations of better in every area of my life. Of course, it does not mean it was a cakewalk or came easy without a faith fight, persecution or troubles. Do not let this turn you away if you are new to Christ. You see, the Bible is clear about what we can expect to encounter as believers in Christ Jesus. The thing to remember is that we are victorious in Christ Jesus.

I found promises in the Word of God that spoke to my situations and the expected outcomes I desired. I used them to formulate affirmations that have led me to where I am now and where I will be going moving forward. The following pages will serve as a form of empowerment if you begin to say it, believe it, imagine it, and thank God for it.

No matter how long it takes for it to manifest, without wavering or doubting, you shall see it, because it is the Word of God. After all, **A Better Me Is For You**[SM].

Affirming My Way To A Better Me

Today, I choose to win or learn, because quitting is not an option.

I will not shut a door that God has opened. I will confidently walk through it in Him, knowing that it is a part of my destiny.

According to Matthew 5:18, I believe that there is no failure in the Word of God. Therefore, I declare that if it is a promise in God's Word for my life, I shall see it manifested in Jesus' Name.

I am valued by God, who has established His worth for my life. I, therefore, will allow myself to be used as a refresher in the lives of those I come in contact with, always leaving the fragrance of His presence in whatever atmosphere I am in. My presence changes the atmosphere, allowing others to be authentic and true to who they are in Christ because my confidence is in Christ Jesus.

A Better Me is For You[SM] – Spiritually

You Say It

The Word tells me that I am fearfully and wonderfully made. The Lord has made me reverential and distinctive. I will demonstrate honor to God as He has made me distinguished. Therefore, my boast will be in Him.

God's love for me and my acceptance of Christ has granted me overwhelming victory in all of life's difficulties. Therefore, I confess that I will not allow life difficulties to burden me. Instead, I will allow myself to declare overwhelming victory. Anything other than victory is non-negotiation.

Romans 8:37 (GWT)

The one who loves us gives us an overwhelming victory in all these difficulties.

God,

I thank You for having me in Your heart when You gave Your only begotten Son for me and all of humanity. No matter what I am faced with, keeping my heart stayed on You, I will endure hardness as a good soldier of Jesus Christ. After all, I am liberated in Christ Jesus and never alone.

Romans 8:30-32 (GWT)

30) He also called those whom he had already appointed. He approved of those whom he had called, and he gave glory to those whom he had approved of.

31) What can we say about all of this? If God is for us, who can be against us?

32) God didn't spare his own Son but handed him over [to death] for all of us. So he will also give us everything along with him.

What I have shared is a snippet of how I began becoming better spiritually on this journey of life. I do not believe that any of us will reach the pinnacle of being our absolute, unequivocally very best. For when we do reach that place, that is to imply we have nothing left to do here on this earth. However, I think we can progress to the position daily by purposefully being better every day of our lives. It involves us knowing who Christ is (out of a personal relationship), knowing who we are in Christ Jesus, and diligently implementing what we know as believers in Christ.

As you read this, your thought may be that you have not given your life to Christ. Your view is perhaps that you are good and do not need to include Him. No matter what it is, there are two things I can assure you – God loves you, and you will gain some wisdom and insight into how loving He is toward us all as you continue to read this book. While I may be sold out for Christ, just like I had to make that decision in my life and for my life, I believe that others must do the same.

As the author of this book, I am sharing some of the things I have done to experience better in every area of my life. And, that which I am sharing, I have absolute proof in my own life of how receiving salvation and applying the Word has given me a level of strength, peace, joy, love, wisdom, patience, and so much more that no matter the fight – I am on the winning side.

Part 2

A Better Me Mentally

When I look at what I have overcome in my life, the most significant was recognizing that I needed to implement God's strategies to overcome challenges. While I have not gone through what others have, without the help of the Lord, it could have been worse. All of our life experiences are different, so I do not think comparing my experiences with others is wise. But because of my life experiences, I diligently pray for others.

Every time I reached a place in my thinking that was not benefiting me, I had to be proactive and get involved in my own breakthrough. Giving others control of our life through our minds is not God's will for our lives or theirs. Now, you may wonder what happened. Instead of sharing the details of what happened, I choose to share what I did to bring change to my life and healing to my mind.

In addition to looking at what we have allowed others to do or say that has plagued our minds with unhealthy thoughts, we must also examine how we make choices. We must examine our lives to see if we are guilty of caring for others and neglecting ourselves – being void of self-care. Proper care of ourselves affords us to serve others better. And, it empowers us to know when to say no, or even to say I cannot currently assist you with that. That in itself can be so liberating.

Overcommitting can lead to stress and anxiety. Stress and anxiety will cause you to perish from your state of living a quality life to one of total depletion. That is not beneficial for us, nor is it helpful for others. Initially, some may not welcome these types of changes coming from you. But, there is no vitality or value in living under stress.

Prioritizing, setting goals, and having order in our lives will lead to a higher quality of life. Spiritually, the proper order is God first and then family. Everything else falls behind these two. After all, our family is our first natural calling/responsibility. So, if we are not in proper order, we will lack total inner peace.

Romans 12:2 GWT

Don't become like the people of this world. Instead, change the way you think. Then you will always be able to determine what God really wants—what is good, pleasing, and perfect.

As a part of my assessment, wanting better and choosing not to be held hostage in the recesses of my mind, I began to look for the things that needed to change to experience the quality of life I desired. Let me say, this may not be where you need to focus. So, as you read what I discovered, take notes and review them to determine what you need to learn, and then put together an action plan to make it happen.

Internalizing the opinions and comments of others added no value to my life. We all have thoughts and can easily comment on something we know or do not know. When you are in a faith fight, the opinions and comments of others in your mind can clutter your thoughts. Protect yourself by not housing the opinion of others in the recess of your mind.

Putting stock in someone else's ideas or thoughts limits your own creative thinking. If you are not careful, you will begin to filter your decisions through their opinion. And, it may be so subtle that you do not realize it until you are too far in. We can end up here when we connect with individuals beyond the intended scope of the relationship.

For instance, the purpose of the connection may be to gleam from, be mentored by, or even become a student. Somewhere and somehow, it went from the ideal goal to you becoming a clone of an individual. Let us be authentic and not become a version of someone else. We need you, your family needs you, and the assignment on your life requires you to show up. Our values increase when we are ourselves. Being authentic eliminates the unnecessary weight of being someone else. It allows me to show up and have no regrets, because I am living my life to please God and enjoy the journey.

Being liberated in Christ Jesus allows me to share there is freedom in the Lord. I made a promise to the Lord that whatever He made known to me to produce overwhelming victory in my life, I would share with others so that they, too, can live a victorious life. Being free of the opinion of others can be so liberating. And, it does not mean that people do not matter to me. However, it does mean they are not my source; God is. And, if He blesses me with them in my life, I will still look to Him as the final authority and not others.

As an influencer, people notice you. This is a great opportunity to let it be known that I am who I am by the grace and favor of God; I am doing what I am doing because of the grace and favor of God. This has led to transformative thinking and how to guide my thoughts in the direction that is beneficial. Having inner peace is refreshing and invigorating. You must begin to see yourself as an overcomer through Christ Jesus and speak words that align with your belief.

Take a moment and examine your thoughts about yourself. Use the questions that follow to help you assess where you are. After doing so, wherever there is evidence of lack or deterioration, be intentional and do something about it to increase your quality of life.

- Do you believe that you are an overcomer?
- Do you believe that you bring value to others?
- Do you value your family without having the mindset of what you have done for me lately?
- Do you have toxic thoughts about yourself and others?
- Is there anyone that you need to forgive?
- When you evaluate your circle, do you need to decrease, increase, or change who's in it?

If you are the brightest one in your group, your circle needs an adjustment. If you bring the least to your group, you need an adjustment. Growth, wisdom, and knowledge add value to our lives.

Manifestations of Better

So much can be written in this segment. I have numerous examples of how my thought life and mental capacity were challenged. But, above the challenge is the outcome of overwhelming victory. We must realize that taking responsibility and ownership of our life derives from our thoughts After this realization, it is important for us to follow up with an action plan.

What you think and say about yourself and others and how you act are all contributing factors to your own wellness. This book will not bring total healing to you mentally. However, I hope it encourages you to go further in the way you take responsibility and ownership of your thoughts. Seek Godly counsel if your church offers pastoral counseling by a licensed professional. Stay in your Word daily, and through the day, quote scriptures.

Know that it is okay to seek a therapist or counselor. If you experience a toothache that has your face throbbing, I will not tell you not to go to a dentist and to just instead pray. I would encourage you to consider requesting an emergency appointment. I would not have to tell you to give them the details of the pain, which side, for how long, etc. You would do that willingly. If you are in a state of depression, regression, oppression, anguish, or any condition that robs you of being mentally sound and stable, be good to yourself, and seek professional help.

God wants you whole, as do others who love and care for you. Yes, there are scriptures about our thought life, just as there are scriptures for our tongue, family, finances, employment, physical health, and so much more. Get the help you need, and you will see that the manifestation of God's promises are far better than any ailment, sickness or disease.

Use the following affirmations to speak change into your mind to change your confessions. Ultimately, you will begin to see a desired change in your life.

Affirming My Way To A Better Me

I intentionally think on things that will have a positive impact on my life and that of others. I will not give anyone control of my life outside of God. I will evaluate connections and partnerships to determine if they are mutually beneficial. I choose to think better and to cast down any thoughts that could lead to sabotage and destruction. I have the mind of Christ.

Decisions that I make can have a long-lasting and life-changing affect. I will weigh the outcome and the options in advance.

Tolerating that which is of no value is not beneficial. I am letting go and adding value to my life.

I am in control of my thoughts of A Better Me!
~ Jasmine Warthen

I declare that my soul is at peace, because I control the narrative of my thoughts, which controls the words that I speak, which causes a shift in the life that I live.

That which is ahead of me is far greater than where I am now. I will not get stuck, but will instead keep moving.

I declare no stress, strain, or struggles within my atmosphere today.

Better than ever is more than a concept to me. It is my daily confession of what I shall see manifested in every area of my life.

You Say It

Since John 8:36 tells me that Christ has set me free, I declare that I am free from bondage, lack, depression, suppression, regression, and anything else that comes to attack my mental state of having and operating with a sound mind in Jesus' Name. So, if the Son sets you free, you will be absolutely free.

John 8:36 (GWT)

So if the Son sets you free, you will be absolutely free.

Father,

I thank You that I have the mind of Christ. I thank You that I am empowered to cast down imaginations and every high thing that exalts itself against the knowledge of Christ.

I choose to be settled in my thought life, refusing to waver or doubt. Your Word says, let not a wavering person think they will receive anything from the Lord, and that which I believe, I shall receive.

I will not be slothful, nor will I live being anxious. As it is settled in heaven, so it is settled in my heart. I will be anxious for nothing, but through prayer and supplication, make my request known unto You. In Jesus' Name, I do pray and give thanks. Amen.

1 Corinthians 2:16 (GWT)

"Who has known the mind of the Lord so that he can teach him?" However, we have the mind of Christ.

2 Corinthians 10:5 (GWT)

and all their intellectual arrogance that oppose the knowledge of God. We take every thought captive so that it is obedient to Christ.

James 1:7 (GWT)

7 A person who has doubts shouldn't expect to receive anything from the Lord.

Romans 12: 11 (GWT)

Don't be lazy in showing your devotion. Use your energy to serve the Lord.

Psalm 119:89 (GWT)

O Lord, your word is established in heaven forever.

Matthew 21:22 (GWT)

Have faith that you will receive whatever you ask for in prayer."

Matthew 6:25 (GWT)

"So I tell you to stop worrying about what you will eat, drink, or wear. Isn't life more than food and the body more than clothes?

Philippians 4:6 (GWT)

Never worry about anything. But in every situation let God know what you need in prayers and requests while giving thanks.

Part 3

A Better Me Physically

Oh my, this part of the journey has been decades in the making. My oldest daughter, Kennetta, recently sent me a picture of me. When I saw the picture, I thought it was my middle daughter, KieVonne. I wondered where she was when she took it. Kennetta then told me that it was me looking like her sister. Of course, we both laughed. As I looked at the picture, I could recall how I felt spiritually, mentally and physically. I was in a great space in these three areas. I was on the other side of a failed marriage and had regained confidence in who I was. This was almost thirty years ago.

Today, where I am, supersedes what I felt then. I am fantastic, empowering, peaceful, joyful and so much more, so much more. And as before, getting to this point, I had to walk through the process to overcome adversities that were different than before.

In December 2019, I was scheduled to have a total hip replacement. The pain resulted from bone-on-bone grinding. According to the medical professionals, only a hip replacement would correct it. I continued to make confessions over my body while preparing for the total hip replacement procedure.

The orthopedic surgeon shared that he wanted to do one more x-ray before the surgery. He was not clear why, but felt it was the right thing to do. Let me tell you that this is one reason my husband and I are always praying for our health professionals. We declare that God will give them His wisdom for our situation. And, that He would provide us with clear directions about our health. We pray for their families, practices, and other patients.

After seeing something he could not identify, he sent me to another specialist, who sent me to a team of doctors. They told my husband and me that it was cancer. They then stated they wanted to do six weeks of chemotherapy followed by another six weeks of radiation, which was then followed by surgery. We were both grateful for all of the doctors and specialists. We even prayed with them as well, and not just for them. And as I said earlier, our prayers were about my life and their other patients.

As grateful as I was to God for them, I would not make any decision without being led by God. And, that is what I would tell anyone to do. Just because I chose a particular route does not mean you should take the same path. My level of faith, trust in God's Word, and being led by God's Spirit were all components of my decisions with my husband's agreement.

I have been a proponent of natural medicine for years, actually decades. I contacted two holistic board-certified doctors, one in the District of Columbia and the other in Pennsylvania. They both almost unanimously gave me the exact instructions of what to do and what not to do. My husband contacted another specialist in South Carolina, and they were providing similar instructions.

I kept declaring the Word of God over my body. I told myself that I would only believe the report of the Lord; I would not die, but live and declare the works of the Lord, and that healing is my portion. I took communion multiple times a day, as often as I thought of it.

In May 2020, the doctor told us the cancer was gone. Though we knew it, because I refused to doubt the Word of God, we celebrated then the way we celebrated before hearing it. By the time I went back in September, it appeared that it had started coming back. The Spirit of God revealed to me that my diet did not change enough. I was eating almost like I used to, and it was not building my body up as it should. This led me to research nutrition and healing, which changed my life.

In October, my primary care physician, who knows I prefer holistic medical care, did one of the most caring and matter-of-fact things for me. She demanded that I see an Oncologist without delay. She insisted that I go see "a real doctor." It was clear that she wanted to make sure I understood the severity of what they saw.

While I believe that there is some great oncologist where I live, it was the response of one person to me when she called to schedule an appointment that made both my husband and I decide that we would go out of town. I began to pray, asking God for guidance; to lead me to medical professionals who believed in natural healing with supplements, diet, and lifestyle changes, and they were board-certified.

My primary care physician wanted to know the names of the ones I was considering so she could also research them. When she called to tell me that after completing her research, she was in absolute agreement with me, all I could do was thank the Lord and then thank her.

I am taking the time to share all of this with you because I want you to believe in God for your healing, good health, and eradication of whatever is ailing you. I want you to ask

God to grant wisdom to the health professionals you see. I want you to declare God's Word, listen to what they tell you, ask questions, and say that healing is my portion after all of that. I want you to focus on what you are believing God for and put in the work to see it manifested. Let me say it again. You must put in the work. Remember that a change is not a change until you change.

Recognize that some people cannot handle hearing about your faith fight. Some may never pray for healing to manifest in my body. You must trust God above everyone else. Listen, my husband and I talked about who we would share information with about our faith fight. We were very selective for two reasons:

1. We wanted those who would agree with our prayers, which were in alignment with the Word of God.

2. One of our sons was preparing to leave the country for an assignment, and the other was not ready to hear this. Nor were many of my other family members. So, we did not want any of them to hear about it without hearing the other side – healing has manifested, and there is no further evidence of disease.

Look, we do not have to tell everything that is going on in our lives. I have chosen to filter my words through one question – Will God get the glory? So I was intentional, by the leading of God's Spirit. My husband and I agreed that with all the devastating news being reported, we were not going to compound it with more. Since we believed in the Good News and that all things are possible because we believed we would not bring any news without good news.

One day at a follow-up appointment, I was asked if I had a prayer group praying for me at my church. Unashamedly, I answered no. They were in shock and asked me why not. I told them that what my husband and I wanted were those who could agree with our prayers, and nothing more unless God gave them something else. We exercised our faith and increased our faith in God's Word over this situation. I did not doubt the Word of God; I was not in fear. And because Ron and I were in agreement with God's Word and one another, we were confident that the Lord was working it out on our behalf.

I also explained that there is so much power in agreement that I did not want people to say they agreed, and then question the process. To me, that is not full agreement. In fact, that begins to chip away at the level of agreement. My final comment was if I could not trust God for what I was believing for, why would I expect someone else to? If others struggle with their belief in God's Word for their lives, especially during a pandemic, why would I expect them to be able to stand in faith with me for my life? I wanted our church and others to hear what God has done so that they, too, can grow in faith to believe that what He has promised is for them as well, but they must believe and not doubt it.

Jeremiah 17:14 (GWT)

Heal me Lord, and I will be healed. Rescue me, and I will be rescued. You are the one I praise.

Exodus 23:25 (GWT)

You must serve the Lord your God, and he will bless your food and water. I will take away all sickness from among you.

Jeremiah 15:16 (GWT)

Your words were found, and I devoured them. Your words are my joy and my heart's delight, because I am called by your name, O Lord God of Armies.

Psalm 30:2 (GWT)

O Lord my God, I cried out to you for help, and you healed me.

Manifestations of Better

I feasted on the scriptures you just read throughout the days, and it continues to be. My husband, led by the Spirit of God, would lay hands, speak to my body and the different systems, and command life and newness. We were in constant prayer, believing and declaring healing for others.

We talked with our daughters in detail and shared with our sons in more general terms initially. They were with us declaring the Word, sending words of healing and encouragement. And, they stood in full agreement with us.

In addition to applying the Word, I changed my diet. I did not find it challenging, because I have practiced vegetarianism in the past. And, a very important factor, I eliminated stress from my life. One of the biggest stressors was multitasking. I was always thinking about the next while doing the now. I went from a stressed life to a committed life of being totally present and fully committing to whatever is now before moving on to the next. As before, we expected to see God's Word manifested in my body. However, this time was different. I spent hours researching, learning what to eat, proper exercises, taking natural supplements with only two prescriptions, getting adequate sleep, and a few other things that have been key to the healing manifesting.

In January 2021, I had a follow-up visit with the oncologist to get a praise report from testing done six weeks prior. Notice, I said we went back for a praise report, because that was/and is where my faith is, and my husband's. Yet again, I experienced the overwhelming victory. God exceeded our expectations. Before hearing the praise report in detail, the oncologist told us that what she was about to share was considered a miracle. Thank You, Lord!

You see, six weeks prior, she reported lesions on the brain. When we returned, they were gone! And, it was not a couple of lesions. Many throughout the brain – but Jehovah Rapha did as His Word said He would – He healed me, and I received the healing. Not only were they gone, but she told us that I was in remission. As she looked at me, she pointed out that where I was sitting, many did not have the same outcome, and she reiterated this is a miracle. Not only did I thank God again for that, but I thanked God for her. On our second visit to her office, we learned she was a woman of faith. The ringtone on her phone and her countenance revealed it to us—another blessing from the Lord.

The one takeaway I want all of you to have is, if you say what you believe, do not doubt it, nor waver in faith, as well as walk and work through the processes in faith to see what you are saying. You shall have what you say. Even if you receive a report that only a tiny percentage of people have beat the odds, you must be willing to tell yourself and live like you are one of the small percentages versus believing the other way around. And the total hip surgery that was to take place did not and no longer needs to happen. ALL PAIN IS GONE. I decree that I have a brand-new body, literally.

In January 2019, I weighed 185 pounds. I experienced a significant decrease from several years, as previously, I weighed 220 pounds. Not only did I change my diet, but I incorporated intermittent fasting and approximately thirty minutes of exercise daily. Today, I weigh in at 159, five dress sizes down. And let me tell you, my appetite has been and remains very strong. My weight loss was not a result of cancer, but because I was intentional about my temple glorifying God. I always had a hearty appetite. Now today, at the revision of this book, I am weighing 145 – my goal weight!

Believing God's Word to be accurate and exercising my faith in God's Word has changed my life literally. Be encouraged and make the necessary changes so that you, too, can have a higher quality of living. Because truly, "***A Better Me Is For You.***SM"

Affirming My Way To A Better Me

I speak to any and all forms of sicknesses and diseases and make it known that you cannot dwell in my body. My body is the temple of the Holy Spirit, and you are in violation of God's promises of healing for my life. I evict and eradicate you now.

I will not be enslaved to junk foods and food binges. I no longer live to eat. I now eat to live. Food is my medicine and a form of cell rejuvenation. It will not be my go-to when I am facing challenges and difficulties – prayer and confession of God's Word will be where I go when facing challenges and difficulties.

I will meditate on the Word of God day and night. Then, I shall make my way prosperous and have good success.

According to scripture, with long life will God satisfy me and show me His salvation.

I will not live in fear of sickness, diseases, man or any form of opposition. I will walk in power, love and with a sound mind.

A Better Me brings victory.
~ Caylin Victoria

I will crush my limitations and keep pushing.
I am closer to where I am going
than where I have been.

You Say It

Fixing our minds on the promises of God has always proven to be effective. The Word in my life is the needful thing. If God said it in His Word, it is so.

1 Corinthians 6:12 (TPT)

It's true that our freedom allows us to do anything, but that doesn't mean that everything we do is good for us. I'm, free to do as I choose, but I choose to never be enslaved to anything.

Proverbs 23:2 (TPT)

Be careful to curb your appetite and catch yourself before you fall into the trap of wanting all you see.

Father,

In Jesus' Name, I declare deliverance from gluttony, flesh pleasing, stress eating, and being enslaved to food. I decree that more will come out of my mouth than that which goes in. I decree that my words will be in alignment with the Word of God.

I see food as medicinal properties above seeing it as a flesh satisfier. Holy Spirit, keep me in the will of the Father, and Jesus, I thank You for making intercession for me.

I am an overcomer by the Blood of the Lamb, and by the words of my testimony in Jesus' Name, I do pray and give thanks, Amen.

Part 4

A Better Me Socially

When our motives are pure, everyone stands to benefit from a social experience. Desiring relationships, companionships, spouses, friends and acquaintances are God-given desires. The Word of God tells us that Abraham was a friend of God and that God walked in the evening with Adam. It also speaks of when Moses spoke to the lamb at the brook, who was thirsty, to say that had he known he was thirsty, he would have carried him on his back. God witnessed the level of compassion Moses had for creatures, which could not compare to His compassion for humans. It got God's attention. Imagine, he demonstrated understanding towards the well-being of a lamb.

When we hear of others taking up causes or fighting for a righteous cause, it is safe to assume they are attracted to and have compassion for those impacted by such a cause. We can name numerous people who have displayed such qualities; Dr. Martin Luther King's assignment came out of compassion, Mother Teresa, Billy Graham, Sojourner Truth, John Lewis, and others we have learned about have taken up social causes.

When I think of others who have served in this capacity, I think of my Mother. I remember how my precious, loving Mother helped others from a heart of compassion and a cause to serve them through education and theater. As I watched her, it seemed the most natural thing to do. To feed those who were hungry, be financially supportive of those who had fallen on tough times, and assist those who God led her to help.

Several years ago, Ronald and I began investing in entrepreneurs who needed capital for their businesses and did not have the means of raising it. The exciting thing is that everyone we agreed to assist were individuals who did not come to us looking for assistance. We learned about some on social media, others due to fellowshipping with them and others via research. The most beautiful thing is that all of the investments have yielded good fruit. They are doing well in their businesses.

We are committed to other causes, but this is one of them for sure. As a business owner, I have had the financial support of my husband and others who support me, such as clients, event attendees and consumers. Our decision to serve others in these various capacities came from a place of compassion to see people succeed in their dreams. Indeed we are blessed to be a blessing.

When my husband and I reconnected in 1995, I was intrigued by so many things about him. One, in particular, was whenever we went to public social gatherings, he made covering me a higher priority than engaging with others full throttle. I asked him about his level of engagement, and his response blessed me. But, it also made me keenly aware of my level of interaction. He would tell me that because I was very engaged in an unfamiliar environment, he was more about being a set of eyes for me so that I could continue to engage and enjoy myself. Well, if you did not know, you have probably figured it out – I enjoy meeting people. It is not that Ron does not, but we have different temperaments. And, our differences balance us out and completes us. We later had a running joke where he would ask me what office I was running for. This was how my Mother was as well.

On a personal level, to have the family that I have (immediate and extended), the friends, and the colleagues, I am truly blessed. I believe that I have the right spouse, children, grandchildren, siblings, in-loves, nieces, nephews, aunties, uncles and cousins. I genuinely believe that. While none of them are perfect, neither am I; I love them all.

In any family, there are challenges that arise. I have purposed to always focus on the victory ahead versus the battles in the moment. And I refuse to rehearse moments of contention unless I am seeking a resolution that begins with self-examination. I believe that if I am aware of a problem, I should be in search of a solution. Otherwise, it is not to occupy my mind or space. That's just my take on issues.

Manifestations of Better

There are many things that I absolutely love about being and bringing who I am and what I have to offer into my relationships and into the social causes that my husband and I support. I say this without arrogance or boasting, but I can say it because I righteously love who I am.

Previously, I stayed away from making such a statement. I realized it was because I did not know my value or worth. I questioned myself, but did not question my motives because they were good. I was once intimidated, insecure, and had an inferior complex. I can tell you that is not me anymore.

Now that I walk in who I am and am comfortable in my skin, I am also good at celebrating, encouraging, esteeming, coaching and empowering others. I am walking in who I am and loving what God has done for me and through me. My confidence remains knowing that He, who has begun a good work in me, is well able to complete it until the return of Christ. This is my confidence that I embrace, and I absolutely love it.

Listen, learn to celebrate yourself, and thank God for the gifts He has given you, how He has kept you, how He uses you, how He has gifted you and so much more. You, too, will realize that I am who I am by the grace of God. Learning to celebrate yourself is a form of empowerment and education on how to engage and initiate the celebration of others.

I am one of the biggest cheerleaders anyone could have, because I am gifted to encourage and empower. I enjoy hearing how others walked through processes to reach their goals and see their dreams come to fruition. Never lose faith or hope, and always remember that you are made to excel and not just to succeed.

2 Corinthians 4:7 (KJV)

But we have this treasure in earthen vessels, that the excellency of the power may be of God, and not of us.

Affirming My Way To A Better Me

I am blessed to have Godly relationships, and they are blessed to have me. We bring value to one another's lives that glorify God.

My social media posts add value to the lives of the readers. I am of Godly character; therefore, I do not embarrass, insult or downgrade others.

I contribute to my community and city that invokes and promotes better for other citizens, not just myself.

I am resourceful and a vessel used by God to assist others in fulfilling their God-given assignment. I am not called to everyone, but I am faithful to God for those I am called to serve, no matter in what capacity.

Maximizing my life does not require me to minimize others.

I bring love and encouragement to my family circle. I declare that my bloodline is living in a matter that is pleasing unto God.

All of my connections are appointed by God, not just for my benefit, but for the benefit of others.

My business attracts the right clients, and my customers' experience exceeds their expectations.

I remain relevant in my purpose by constantly learning from reading, research, continuing education, recertifications and industry connections.

I do not plagiarize or take from others, because God has gifted me; therefore, I am creative.

I stand out, and I stand strong amongst my colleagues, influencers, and mentors, which is a reflection of who I am and who they are.

You Say It

Here are a few questions to ask about the relationships you build:

- What do you desire out of your relationships?
- What are the expectations of the connections from the other parties?
- Do you all have known boundaries that you should agree upon?
- Have you all established the purpose, benefit, and desired goals that you want to accomplish in the relationship?

If you are thinking about getting married or are married, I encourage you to use the above questions as a guide. Go into every relationship with expectations. Knowing what both parties want can help you recognize the level of commitment and work involved in reaching those goals.

One of my best friends keeps me laughing. Our relationship is deeper than laughter, and we both have an expectation when we connect. When I share with Ron our text messages or conversations that keep me laughing, he finds himself laughing, too. Oftentimes, this is followed by, "That's what I expect from you two". I love it – laughter is great therapy for your soul, and it promotes healing in your body.

Proverbs 18:24 (GWT)

Friends can destroy one another, but a loving friend can stick closer than family.

Father,

You value relationships. That is why You sent Your Son to be a propitiation for our sins, even that of the whole world. You made us in Your image and after Your likeness.

You did not create any of us to be alone, in isolation, or live in solitary confinement. All of those things are a form of imprisonment. Instead, You have given us freedom, for Whom the Son has set free is free indeed. I decree I am a partaker of Your grace and a giver of it as well.

I embrace every God-ordained relationship established by You for my life. I also will not allow those relationships to impede or destroy my relationship with You or with the order You have established for my family.

Let me recognize when You are mandating a shift in these relationships and follow You as Holy Spirit leads. Whether the shift is to increase the capacity to bond closer or to recognize that a relationship has run it's course, and/or it is necessary to redefine it. This I pray for Your glory in Jesus' Name. I thank You. Amen.

Part 5

A Better Me Financially

Every day, we all give something, whether our opinion, putting words in the atmosphere or giving love. No matter what it is, there is an exchange. When we give our opinion, someone can exchange it for agreement or disagreement (whether spoken or implied). The words that we release are empowered into action, whether we intend to or not. And, when giving love, we get it back in great abundance. Also, there is certainly nothing wrong with sowing as led by the Lord.

The leading from the Lord should also be in our finances – saving, spending, sowing and splurging. Some of you may have pulled back from sowing, and others may splurge from not exercising discipline in your spending, and that is why you are having financial challenges – you are not sowing (giving) according to the Word of God. Those of you struggling with splurging must know when to splurge and how much you can afford.

Listen, I have experienced the lack – self-inflicted and economy inflicted. And, neither one was pleasurable nor desired. I had to put the work in to transition from scarcity to more than enough and from more than enough to a beautiful level of abundance.

One principle my husband and I have been diligent in living by is that of a generous giver. Sowing far more than the 10%

of our tithe and reaping a continual harvest. Thank You, Lord!

I would not share anything as a suggestion for others to do if I was not a partaker and got great results. You may be experiencing a level of excellence without giving, but imagine how much greater it would be if you did give. You would reach another level of excellence; the only way to know it is to try it.

Financial literacy is a position we should strive to achieve. We need to know that having the best and being the best is not for an elite few. God wants that for all of us. But, as my husband frequently says, "We have to be willing participants in our breakthrough." Yes, our breakthrough does require our involvement. There are four things you can do now to improve your financial position:

- Sow according to scripture – at least 10% (Leviticus 27:30)

- Save at a minimum of 10% until you have reached $1,000, and then your next goal is three, six, and twelve months of monthly expenses.

- Slay debt. I recommend the snowball method, paying off the smallest amount first so you can quickly see progress.

- Spend with a budget in operation so you can have a better financial life in the future.

You can do all of this using a budget. As a life coach, I have seen the quality of life for others explode, as well as in our lives.

Learn what you like and plan for it. As an example, if you do not want the work of having a swimming pool, using a swimming pool, why have one built? What do you gain from having one, because someone else has one? Taking others out of the equation will free you up to live the life you want to live. After all, many could care less about seeing you with those things. So, is it worth the expense just for others to know you have what you have? I think not.

There is rarely a day that goes by when I do not thank God and my husband for our home. It is so us. I love being home and enjoying nature around me. Even now, as I write, I am outside on my veranda. You may wonder or think it is a mansion. However, it is not by your definition. It's my mansion, because I love being here. The bottom line is to live your life as you truly desire, pleasing God with the things and people you enjoy.

Manifestations of Better

- No matter how big or small, celebrate every accomplishment toward your financial literacy goals.
- Delayed self-gratification is a form of empowerment and encouragement. You will achieve results.
- Having the capacity for more comes from having the freedom of less debt.
- The decisions you make in life are long-lasting and life-changing.

What level of expectation do you have for yourself? Do you believe what you genuinely desire is for others and not for you? Do you think that your past is a determining factor for your future? Do you wish and hope versus dream and plan? Today make a conscientious decision to change, beginning with answering these questions:

- Why would I reject the plan of God for my life, which includes prosperity and good health?

- Why am I allowing my past to hold me hostage when God has forgiven me, and I am in my present, heading to my future?

- Why would I allow wishing and hoping to impede me from seeing my dreams planned out for manifestation?

Affirming My Way To A Better Me

I declare that every seed sown as a generous giver in the Kingdom of God, as a philanthropist, and as an investor will produce a bountiful harvest not just for me, but for my family, my church, and my community.

My word is my bond and a reflection of my Godly character. And because I keep my word, I can declare and decree a thing, and it shall be established according to Job 22:28.

God can afford my dreams. I will create a plan that is led by Holy Spirit and execute every phase of it until it comes into full manifestation.

Greater is the Lord who is in me than he who is in the world.

I am a kingdom paymaster living an abundant life through the manifested promises of God.

My end is far greater and more rewarding than my beginning.

No matter what challenges arise, I have, by faith, already overcome them.

I am a repairer of the breach and a billboard for the Lord of how using His principle yields higher dividends and results.

You Say It

I am who I say I am, as I say who He says I am. I am living the abundant life, full of the manifested promises of God.

It is He that gives me the power to obtain wealth. I, therefore, allow Him to order my steps toward others.

I am a generational wealth builder, leaving an inheritance to my family, including faith, favor, finances and forever seekers of Jesus Christ.

Just as God has led and blessed me to be a part of my church, I demonstrate my gratitude in serving, sowing and submission.

Part 6

Conclusion

It has been such a joy to write this book. I know that living a better life will lead to living our best life, which can only be done through Christ Jesus. And, the best is not from the perspective that we have arrived, but from the perspective that my "betters" will become the sum of my best when I have passed from this life to my next in Christ Jesus. However, we must not despise small beginnings. It is incumbent upon us to perfect ourselves on every level to bring and be the best version of ourselves that we can be.

God has already done for you and me, and we must remember that He is no respecter of person. In principle, what He has done for one, He will do for others. Nevertheless, we must be willing participants and recipients of His grace and plan for our lives.

Purpose to live better in every area of your life. We can do it, because we are more than conquerors in Christ Jesus. Never see challenges as a death sentence or a stop-all gap. Change your perspective and see it as an opportunity for God's Word to work in your life. See it as a part of your life journey en route to A Better Me. See it with endless opportunities to perfect yourself and to bless others.

I am fully committed to being all God has called me to be. I am equally committed to enjoying the journey. We miss significant moments and opportunities when we think and walk as if we are defeated. My brothers and sisters, I am cheering you on to spiritual maturity, mental and physical health, social involvement and financial literacy. After all, ***A Better Me Is For You***SM!

There is an untapped well of empowerment in you. Dive in.
~ Desiree V. Johnson

My life is better than ever, and we are still moving forward.

Author's Notes

PASTOR | MASTER CERTIFIED LIFE COACH
HOLISTIC HEALTH COACH AND CONSULTANT

Angela M. Scott
A Better Me Empowerment
www.itsabetterme.org.
contact@itsabetterme.org
Social Media: A Better Me Empowerment

ZCP
ZYIA CHRISTIAN PUBLISHING

www.ingramcontent.com/pod-product-compliance
Ingram Content Group UK Ltd.
Pitfield, Milton Keynes, MK11 3LW, UK
UKHW060358300726
14090UKWH00001B/12

* 9 7 9 8 2 1 8 1 8 4 4 5 2 *